THOMAS AND BEULAH

Books by Rita Dove

The Yellow House on the Corner
Museum
Fifth Sunday (short stories)
Thomas and Beulah

Limited Editions

Ten Poems
The Only Dark Spot in the Sky
Mandolin

THOMAS AND BEULAH

poems by

Rita Dove

Carnegie-Mellon University Press
Pittsburgh 1986

ACKNOWLEDGMENTS

These poems have appeared, sometimes in different versions, in the following magazines:

Agni Review ("Daystar," "Weathering Out"); *Callaloo* ("Company," "The House on Bishop Street," "Motherhood," "Nightmare," "One Volume Missing," "Promises," "Recovery," "Roast Possum," "Straw Hat," "Under the Viaduct, 1932"); *Cutbank* ("Aircraft," "Obedience"); *Georgia Review* ("Gospel"); *New England Review & Bread Loaf Quarterly* ("Courtship, Diligence," "The Oriental Ballerina"); *Nimrod* ("Magic," "Sunday Greens"); *Paris Review* ("Lightnin' Blues," "The Satisfaction Coal Company," "Wingfoot Lake"); *Ploughshares* ("Taking in Wash"); *Poetry* ("Pomade"); *The Reaper* ("A Hill of Beans," "Nothing Down," "Thomas at the Wheel").

The following poems appeared as a chapbook feature under the title *Mandolin* in *Ohio Review 28*: "The Event," "Variation on Pain," "Jiving," "The Zeppelin Factory," "Courtship," "Refrain," "Variation on Guilt," "Compendium," "Definition in the Face of Unnamed Fury," "Aurora Borealis," "The Charm," and "The Stroke."

"The Great Palaces of Versailles," "Pomade," and "The Oriental Ballerina" appeared in *New American Poets of the Eighties* (Wampeter Press, 1984). "Dusting" first appeared in *Poetry* and subsequently in *Pushcart Prize: VII* (Pushcart Press, 1982), *Museum* (Carnegie-Mellon University Press, 1983), and *The Morrow Anthology of Younger American Poets* (1985).

"A Hill of Beans" and "Wingfoot Lake" also appeared in *The Bread Loaf Anthology of Contemporary American Poetry* (University Press of New England, 1985).

I wish to thank the John Simon Guggenheim Memorial Foundation for a fellowship which enabled me to complete this book. I am also grateful to Arizona State University for supporting this project through a faculty grant.

The publication of this book is supported by grants from the National Endowment for the Arts in Washington, D.C., a Federal agency, and from the Pennsylvania Council on the Arts.

Library of Congress Catalog Card Number 85-71965
ISBN 0-88748-020-9
ISBN 0-88748-021-7 pbk.

for my mother, Elvira Elizabeth

**These poems tell two sides of a story
and are meant to be read in sequence.**

Contents

I. Mandolin

The Event / 11
Variation on Pain / 13
Jiving / 14
Straw Hat / 15
Courtship / 16
Refrain / 18
Variation on Guilt / 20
Nothing Down / 21
The Zeppelin Factory / 24
Under the Viaduct, 1932 / 26
Lightnin' Blues / 27
Compendium / 28
Definition in the Face of Unnamed Fury / 29
Aircraft / 30
Aurora Borealis / 31
Variation on Gaining a Son / 32
One Volume Missing / 33
The Charm / 34
Gospel / 35
Roast Possum / 37
The Stroke / 39
The Satisfaction Coal Company / 40
Thomas at the Wheel / 43

II. Canary in Bloom

Taking in Wash / 47
Magic / 48
Courtship, Diligence / 50
Promises / 51
Dusting / 52
A Hill of Beans / 54
Weathering Out / 56
Motherhood / 58
Anniversary / 59
The House on Bishop Street / 60
Daystar / 61
Obedience / 62
The Great Palaces of Versailles / 63
Pomade / 65
Headdress / 67
Sunday Greens / 69
Recovery / 70
Nightmare / 71
Wingfoot Lake / 72
Company / 74
The Oriental Ballerina / 75

Chronology / 78

I

MANDOLIN

Black Boy, O Black Boy,
is the port worth the cruise?

— *Melvin B. Tolson,*
Harlem Gallery

The Event

Ever since they'd left the Tennessee ridge
with nothing to boast of
but good looks and a mandolin,

the two Negroes leaning
on the rail of a riverboat
were inseparable: Lem plucked

to Thomas' silver falsetto.
But the night was hot and they were drunk.
They spat where the wheel

churned mud and moonlight,
they called to the tarantulas
down among the bananas

to come out and dance.
You're so fine and mighty; let's see
what you can do, said Thomas, pointing

to a tree-capped island.
Lem stripped, spoke easy: *Them's chestnuts,*
I believe. Dove

quick as a gasp. Thomas, dry
on deck, saw the green crown shake
as the island slipped

you have to dive
to see the rest

Thomas BF, Lem drowns

under, dissolved
in the thickening stream.
At his feet

a stinking circle of rags,
the half-shell mandolin.
Where the wheel turned the water

gently shirred.

Variation on Pain

Two strings, one pierced cry.
So many ways to imitate
The ringing in his ears.

He lay on the bunk, mandolin
In his arms. Two strings
For each note and seventeen
Frets; ridged sound
Humming beneath calloused
Fingertips.

There was a needle
In his head but nothing
Fit through it. Sound quivered
Like a rope stretched clear
To land, tensed and brimming,
A man gurgling air.

Two greased strings
For each pierced lobe:
So is the past forgiven.

Jiving

Heading North, straw hat
cocked on the back of his head,

tight curls gleaming
with brilliantine, he didn't stop

until the nights of chaw
and river-bright

had retreated, somehow
into another's life. He landed

in Akron, Ohio
1921,

on the dingy beach
of a man-made lake.

Since what he'd been through
he was always jiving, gold hoop

from the right ear jiggling
and a glass stud, bright blue

in his left. The young ladies
saying *He sure plays*

that tater bug
like the devil!

sighing their sighs
and dimpling.

Straw Hat

In the city, under the saw-toothed leaves of an oak
overlooking the tracks, he sits out
the last minutes before dawn, lucky
to sleep third shift. Years before
he was anything, he lay on
so many kinds of grass, under stars,
the moon's bald eye opposing.

He used to sleep like a glass of water
held up in the hand of a very young girl.
Then he learned he wasn't perfect, that
no one was perfect. So he made his way
North under the bland roof of a tent
too small for even his lean body.

The mattress ticking he shares in the work barracks
is brown and smells
from the sweat of two other men.
One of them chews snuff:
he's never met either.
To him, work is a narrow grief
and the music afterwards
is like a woman
reaching into his chest
to spread it around. When he sings

he closes his eyes.
He never knows when she'll be coming
but when she leaves, he always
tips his hat.

Courtship

1.

Fine evening may I have
the pleasure...
up and down the block
waiting — for what? A
magnolia breeze, someone
to trot out the stars?

But she won't set a foot
in his turtledove Nash,
it wasn't proper.
Her pleated skirt fans
softly, a circlet of arrows.

King of the Crawfish
in his yellow scarf,
mandolin belly pressed tight
to his hounds-tooth vest —
his wrist flicks for the pleats
all in a row, sighing...

2.

...so he wraps the yellow silk
still warm from his throat
around her shoulders. (He made
good money; he could buy another.)
A gnat flies
in his eye and she thinks
he's crying.

Then the parlor festooned
like a ship and Thomas
twirling his hat in his hands
wondering how did I get here.
China pugs guarding a fringed settee
where a father, half-Cherokee,
smokes and frowns.
I'll give her a good life —
what was he doing,
selling all for a song?
His heart fluttering shut
then slowly opening.

Refrain

The man inside the mandolin
plays a new tune
every night, sailing
past the bedroom window:

Take a gourd and string it
Take a banana and peel it
Buy a baby blue Nash
And wheel and deal it

Now he's raised a mast
and tied himself to it
with rags, drunker
than a robin on the wing:

Count your kisses
Sweet as honey
Count your boss'
Dirty money

The bed's oak
and clumsy, pitching
with its crew,
a man and a wife —

Now he's dancing, moving
only his feet. No way
to shut him up but
roll over, scattering

ruffles and silk,
stiff with a dog's breath
among lilies
and ripening skin:

Love on a raft
By the light o' the moon
And the bandit gaze
Of the old raccoon.

Variation on Guilt

Count it anyway he wants —
by the waiting room clock,
by a lengthening hangnail,
by his buttons, the cigars crackling
in cellophane —

no explosion. No latch clangs
home. Perfect bystander, high
and dry with a scream caught
in his throat, he looks down

the row of faces coddled
in anxious pride. Wretched
little difference, he thinks,
between enduring pain and
waiting for pain
to work on others.

The doors fly apart — no,
he wouldn't run away!
It's a girl, he can tell
by that smirk, that strut of a mountebank!

But he doesn't feel a thing.
Weak with rage,
Thomas deals the cigars,
spits out the bitter tip in tears.

Nothing Down

He lets her pick the color.
She saunters along the gleaming fenders
trying to guess his mind.

> *The flower*
> *dangled, blue flame*
> *above his head.*
> *He had stumbled into the woods*
> *and found this silent*
> *forgiveness.*

How they'd all talk!
Punkin and Babe,
Willemma tsk-tsking in her
sinking cabin,

> *a child's forest,*
> *moss and threads*
> *gone wild with hope*

the boys down by the creek
grown now, straddling
the rail at the General Store...

> *Lem smiled from a tree*
> *and nodded when Thomas told him*
> *he was a few years early.*
> *"We'll run away together,"*
> *was all Lem said.*

She bends over,
admiring her reflection
in the headlamp casing of a Peerless.

> *On an ordinary day*
> *he would have plucked this*
> *blue trumpet of Heaven*
> *and rushed it home to water.*

"Nigger Red,"
she drawls, moving on.

> *"Catching a woman," Lem used*
> *to say, "is like rubbing*
> *two pieces of silk together.*
> *Done right, the sheen jags*
> *and the grit shines through."*

A sky blue Chandler!
She pauses, feeling his gaze.

> *Every male on the Ridge*
> *old enough to whistle*
> *was either in the woods*
> *or under a porch.*
> *He could hear the dogs*
> *rippling up the hill.*

Eight miles outside Murfreesboro
the burn of stripped rubber,
soft mud of a ditch.
A carload of white men
halloo past them on Route 231.
"You and your South!" she shouts
above the radiator hiss.
"Don't tell me this ain't what
you were hoping for."

> *The air was being torn*
> *into hopeless pieces.*
> *Only this flower hovering*
> *above his head*
> *couldn't hear the screaming.*
> *That is why the petals had grown*
> *so final.*

The Zeppelin Factory

The zeppelin factory
needed workers, all right —
but, standing in the cage
of the whale's belly, sparks
flying off the joints
and noise thundering,
Thomas wanted to sit
right down and cry.

That spring the third
largest airship was dubbed
the biggest joke
in town, though they all
turned out for the launch.
Wind caught,
"The Akron" floated
out of control,

three men in tow —
one dropped
to safety, one
hung on but the third,
muscles and adrenalin
failing, fell
clawing
six hundred feet.

Thomas at night
in the vacant lot:
*Here I am, intact
and faint-hearted.*

Thomas hiding
his heart with his hat
at the football game, eyeing
the Goodyear blimp overhead:
*Big boy I know
you're in there.*

Under the Viaduct, 1932

He avoided the empty millyards,
the households towering
next to the curb. It was dark
where he walked, although above him
the traffic was hissing.

He poked a trail in the mud
with his tin-capped stick.
If he had a son this time
he would teach him how to step
between his family and the police,
the mob bellowing
as a kettle of communal soup
spilled over a gray bank of clothes....

The pavement wobbled, loosened by rain.
He liked it down here
where the luck of the mighty
had tumbled,

black suit and collarbone.
He could smell the worms stirring in their holes.
He could watch the white sheet settle
while all across the North Hill Viaduct

tires slithered to a halt.

Lightnin' Blues

On the radio a canary bewailed her luck
while the county outside was kicking with rain.
The kids bickered in the back seat;
the wife gasped whenever lightning struck
where it damn well pleased. Friday night,

and he never sang better. The fish
would be flashing like beautiful sequined cigars.
This time he'd fixed the bait himself,
cornmeal and a little sugar water
stirred to a ball on the stove,
pinched off for the scavenger carp.

So why did the car stall? And leap
backwards every time he turned the key?
Was Gabriel a paper man, a horn player
who could follow only the notes on the score?
Or was this sheriff the culprit,
pressing his badge to the window to say
You're lucky — a tree fell on the road ahead
just a few minutes ago.

Turned around, the car started
meek as a lamb. No one spoke
but that old trickster on the radio,
Kingfish addressing the Mystic Knights of the Sea.

Compendium

He gave up fine cordials and
his hounds-tooth vest.

He became a sweet tenor
in the gospel choir.

Canary, usurper
of his wife's affections.

Girl girl
girl girl.

In the parlor, with streamers,
a bug on a nail.

The canary courting its effigy.
The girls fragrant in their beds.

Definition in the Face of Unnamed Fury

That dragonfly, bloated, pinned
to the wall, its gossamer wings in tatters
(yellow silk, actually, faded in rivulets) —
what is it? A pendulum
with time on its hands, a frozen
teardrop, a winter melon
with a white, sweet flesh?

Go on — ask the canary.
Ask that sun-bleached delicacy
in its house of sticks
and it will answer *Pelican's bill.*
What else did you expect?

"How long has it been...?"
Too long. Each note slips
into querulous rebuke, fingerpads
scored with pain, shallow ditches
to rut in like a runaway slave
with a barking heart. Days afterwards
blisters to hide from the children.
Hanging by a thread. *Some day,*
he threatens, *I'll just*
let go.

Aircraft

Too frail for combat, he stands
before an interrupted wing,
playing with an idea, nothing serious.
Afternoons, the hall gaped with aluminum
glaring, flying toward the sun; now
though, first thing in the morning, there is only
gray sheen and chatter
from the robust women around him
and the bolt waiting for his riveter's
five second blast.

The night before in the dark
of the peanut gallery, he listened to blouses shifting
and sniffed magnolias, white
tongues of remorse
sinking into the earth. Then
the newsreel leapt forward
into war.

Why *frail*? Why not simply
family man? Why wings, when
women with fingers no smaller than his
dabble in the gnarled intelligence of an engine?

And if he gave just a four second blast,
or three? Reflection is such

a bloodless light.
After lunch, they would bathe in fire.

Aurora Borealis

This far south such crippling
Radiance. People surge
From their homes onto the streets, certain
This is the end,
For it is 1943
And they are tired.

Thomas walks out of the movie house
And forgets where he is.
He is drowning and
The darkness above him
Spits and churns.

What shines is a thought
Which has lost its way. Helpless
It hangs and shivers
Like a veil. So much

For despair.
Thomas, go home.

Variation on Gaining a Son

That shy angle of his daughter's head —
where did they all learn it?
And her soldier at tender attention,
waiting for the beloved to slide out
beneath the veil. Thomas knew

what he'd find there — a mocking smile, valiant
like that on the smooth face of the young sergeant
drilled neatly through the first minute of battle.
Women called it *offering up a kiss.*

He watched the bridegroom swallow.
For the first time Thomas felt like
calling him *Son.*

One Volume Missing

Green sludge of a riverbank,
swirled and blotched,
as if a tree above him were shuffling
cards.
    Who would have thought
the binding of a "Standard Work
of Reference in the Arts,
Science, History, Discovery
and Invention" could bring back

slow afternoons with a line and bent nail

here, his wingtips balanced
on a scuffed linoleum square
at the basement rummage sale
of the A.M.E. Zion Church?

He opens *Motherwell-Orion* and finds
orchids on the frontispiece
overlain with tissue,
fever-specked and drooping
their enflamed penises.

Werner's Encyclopedia,
Akron, Ohio, 1909:
Complete in Twenty-Five Volumes
minus one —

for five bucks
no zebras, no Virginia,
no wars.

The Charm

They called us
the tater bug twins.
We could take a tune
and chew it up, fling
it to the moon
for the crows to eat.

At night he saw him,
naked and swollen
under the backyard tree.
No reason, he replied
when asked why he'd done
it. Thomas woke up
minutes later, thinking
What I need is a drink.

Sunday mornings
fried fish and hominy steaming
from the plates like an oracle.
The canary sang more furious
than ever, but he heard
the whisper: *I ain't dead.*
I just gave you my life.

Gospel

Swing low so I
can step inside —
a humming ship of voices
big with all

the wrongs done
done them.
No sound this generous
could fail:

ride joy until
it cracks like an egg,
make sorrow
seethe and whisper.

From a fortress
of animal misery
soars the chill voice
of the tenor, enraptured

with sacrifice.
What do I see,
he complains, notes
brightly rising

towards a sky
blank with promise.
Yet how healthy
the single contralto

settling deeper
into her watery furs!
Carry me home,
she cajoles, bearing

down. Candelabras
brim. But he slips
through God's net and swims
heavenward, warbling.

Roast Possum

The possum's a greasy critter
that lives on persimmons and what
the Bible calls carrion.
So much from the 1909 Werner
Encyclopedia, three rows of deep green
along the wall. A granddaughter
propped on each knee,
Thomas went on with his tale —

but it was for Malcolm, little
Red Delicious, that he invented
embellishments: *We shined that possum*
with a torch and I shinnied up,
being the smallest,
to shake him down. He glared at me,
teeth bared like a shark's
in that torpedo snout.
Man he was tough but no match
for old-time know-how.

Malcolm hung back, studying them
with his gold hawk eyes. When the girls
got restless, Thomas talked horses:
Strolling Jim, who could balance
a glass of water on his back
and trot the village square
without spilling a drop. Who put
Wartrace on the map and was buried
under a stone, like a man.

They liked that part.
He could have gone on to tell them

that the Werner admitted Negro children
to be intelligent, though briskness
clouded over at puberty, bringing
indirection and laziness. Instead,
he added: *You got to be careful*
with a possum when he's on the ground;
he'll turn on his back and play dead
till you give up looking. That's
what you'd call sullin'.

Malcolm interrupted to ask
who owned Strolling Jim,
and who paid for the tombstone.
They stared each other down
man to man, before Thomas,
as a grandfather, replied:
                              Yessir,
we enjoyed that possum. We ate him
real slow, with sweet potatoes.

The Stroke

Later he'll say Death stepped right up
to shake his hand, then squeezed
until he sank to his knees. *(Get up,*
nigger. Get up and try again.)

Much later he'll admit he'd been afraid,
curled tight in the center of the rug, sunlight
striking one cheek and plaited raffia
scratching the other. He'll leave out

the part about daydream's aromatic fields
and the strap-worn flanks of the mule
he followed through them. When his wife asks
how did it feel, he won't mention

that the sun shone like the summer
she was pregnant with their first, and
that she craved watermelon which he smuggled
home wrapped in a newspaper, and how

the bus driver smirked as his nickel
clicked through — no, he'll say
it was like being kicked by a mule.
Right now, though, pinned to the bull's-eye,

he knows it was Lem all along:
Lem's knuckles tapping his chest in passing,
Lem's heart, for safekeeping,
he shores up in his arms.

The Satisfaction
Coal Company

1.

What to do with a day.
Leaf through *Jet*. Watch T.V.
Freezing on the porch
but he goes anyhow, snow too high
for a walk, the ice treacherous.
Inside, the gas heater takes care of itself;
he doesn't even notice being warm.

Everyone says he looks great.
Across the street a drunk stands smiling
at something carved in a tree.
The new neighbor with the floating hips
scoots out to get the mail
and waves once, brightly,
storm door clipping her heel on the way in.

2.

Twice a week he had taken the bus down Glendale hill
to the corner of Market. Slipped through
the alley by the canal and let himself in.
Started to sweep
with terrible care, like a woman
brushing shine into her hair,
same motion, same lullaby.
No curtains — the cop on the beat
stopped outside once in the hour
to swing his billy club and glare.

It was better on Saturdays
when the children came along:
he mopped while they emptied
ashtrays, clang of glass on metal
then a dry scutter. Next they counted
nailheads studding the leather cushions.
Thirty-four! they shouted,
that was the year and
they found it mighty amusing.

But during the week he noticed more —
lights when they gushed or dimmed
at the Portage Hotel, the 10:32
picking up speed past the B & O switchyard,
floorboards trembling and the explosive
kachook kachook kachook kachook
and the oiled rails ticking underneath.

3.

They were poor then but everyone had been poor.
He hadn't minded the sweeping,
just the thought of it — like now
when people ask him what he's thinking
and he says *I'm listening.*

Those nights walking home alone,
the bucket of coal scraps banging his knee,
he'd hear a roaring furnace
with its dry, familiar heat. Now the nights
take care of themselves — as for the days,

there is the canary's sweet curdled song,
the wino smiling through his dribble.
Past the hill, past the gorge
choked with wild sumac in summer,
the corner has been upgraded.
Still, he'd like to go down there someday
to stand for a while, and get warm.

Thomas at the Wheel

This, then, the river he had to swim.
Through the wipers the drugstore
shouted, lit up like a casino,
neon script leering from the shuddering asphalt.

Then the glass doors flew apart
and a man walked out to the curb
to light a cigarette. Thomas thought
the sky was emptying itself as fast
as his chest was filling with water.

Should he honk? What a joke —
he couldn't ungrip the steering wheel.
The man looked him calmly in the eye
and tossed the match away.

And now the street dark, not a soul
nor its brother. He lay down across
the seat, a pod set to sea,
a kiss unpuckering. He watched
the slit eye of the glove compartment,
the prescription inside,

he laughed as he thought *Oh
the writing on the water.* Thomas imagined
his wife as she awoke missing him,
cracking a window. He heard sirens
rise as the keys swung, ticking.

II

CANARY IN BLOOM

Ah, how the senses flood at my repeating,
As once in her fire-lit heart I felt the furies
Beating, beating.

    — Anne Spencer,
    "Lines to a Nasturtium"

Taking in Wash

Papa called her Pearl when he came home
drunk, swaying as if the wind touched
only him. Towards winter his skin paled,
buckeye to ginger root, cold drawing
the yellow out. The Cherokee in him,
Mama said. Mama never changed:
when the dog crawled under the stove
and the back gate slammed, Mama hid
the laundry. Sheba barked as she barked
in snow or clover, a spoiled and ornery bitch.

She was Papa's girl,
black though she was. Once,
in winter, she walked through a dream
all the way down the stairs
to stop at the mirror, a beast
with stricken eyes
who screamed the house awake. Tonight

every light hums, the kitchen arctic
with sheets. Papa is making the hankies
sail. Her foot upon a silk
stitched rose, she waits
until he turns, his smile sliding all over.
Mama a tight dark fist.
Touch that child

and I'll cut you down
just like the cedar of Lebanon.

Magic

Practice makes perfect, the old folks said.
So she rehearsed deception
until ice cubes
dangled willingly
from a plain white string
and she could change
an egg into her last nickel.
Sent to the yard to sharpen,

she bent so long over
the wheel the knives
grew thin. When she stood up,
her brow shorn clean
as a wheatfield and
stippled with blood,
she felt nothing, even
when Mama screamed.

She fed sauerkraut to the apple tree;
the apples bloomed tarter
every year. Like all art
useless and beautiful, like
sailing in air,

things happened
to her. One night she awoke
and on the lawn blazed
a scaffolding strung in lights.
Next morning the Sunday paper
showed the Eiffel Tower
soaring through clouds.
It was a sign

she would make it to Paris one day.

Courtship, Diligence

A yellow scarf runs through his fingers
as if it were melting.
Thomas dabbing his brow.

And now his mandolin in a hurry
though the night, as they say,
is young,
though she is *getting on.*

Hush, the strings tinkle. *Pretty gal.*

Cigar-box music!
She'd much prefer a pianola
and scent in a sky-colored flask.

Not that scarf, bright as butter.
Not his hands, cool as dimes.

Promises

*Each hurt swallowed
is a stone.* Last words
whispered to his daughter
as he placed her fingertips
lightly into the palm
of her groom.

She smiled upwards
to Jesus, then Thomas,
turning her back as
politely as possible.
If that were the case
he was a mountain of shame.

Poised on the stone
steps of the church,
she tried to forget
his hulk in the vestibule,
clumsy in blue serge,
his fingers worrying the
lucky bead in his pocket.

Beneath the airborne bouquet
was a meadow of virgins
urging *Be water, be light.*
A deep breath, and she plunged
through sunbeams and kisses,
rice drumming
the both of them blind.

Dusting

Every day a wilderness — no
shade in sight. Beulah
patient among knicknacks,
the solarium a rage
of light, a grainstorm
as her gray cloth brings
dark wood to life.

Under her hand scrolls
and crests gleam
darker still. What
was his name, that
silly boy at the fair with
the rifle booth? And his kiss and
the clear bowl with one bright
fish, rippling
wound!

Not Michael —
something finer. Each dust
stroke a deep breath and
the canary in bloom.
Wavery memory: home
from a dance, the front door
blown open and the parlor
in snow, she rushed
the bowl to the stove, watched
as the locket of ice
dissolved and he
swam free.

That was years before
Father gave her up
with her name, years before
her name grew to mean
Promise, then
Desert-in-Peace.
Long before the shadow and
sun's accomplice, the tree.

Maurice.

A Hill of Beans

One spring the circus gave
free passes and there was music,
the screens unlatched
to let in starlight. At the well,
a monkey tipped her his fine red hat
and drank from a china cup.
By mid-morning her cobblers
were cooling on the sill.
Then the tents folded and the grass

grew back with a path
torn waist-high to the railroad
where the hoboes jumped the slow curve
just outside Union Station.
She fed them while they talked,
easy in their rags. *Any two points*
make a line, they'd say,
and we're gonna ride them all.

Cat hairs
came up with the dipper;
Thomas tossed on his pillow
as if at sea. When money failed
for peaches, she pulled
rhubarb at the edge of the field.
Then another man showed up
in her kitchen and she smelled
fear in his grimy overalls,
the pale eyes bright as salt.

There wasn't even pork
for the navy beans. But he ate
straight down to the blue
bottom of the pot and rested
there a moment, hardly breathing.
That night she made Thomas
board up the well.
Beyond the tracks, the city blazed
as if looks were everything.

Weathering Out

She liked mornings the best — Thomas gone
to look for work, her coffee flushed with milk,

outside autumn trees blowsy and dripping.
Past the seventh month she couldn't see her feet

so she floated from room to room, houseshoes flapping,
navigating corners in wonder. When she leaned

against a door jamb to yawn, she disappeared entirely.

Last week they had taken a bus at dawn
to the new airdock. The hangar slid open in segments

and the zeppelin nosed forward in its silver envelope.
The man walked it out gingerly, like a poodle,

then tied it to a mast and went back inside.
Beulah felt just that large and placid, a lake;

she glistened from cocoa butter smoothed in
when Thomas returned every evening nearly

in tears. He'd lean an ear on her belly
and say: *Little fellow's really talking,*

though to her it was more the *pok-pok-pok*
of a fingernail tapping a thick cream lampshade.

Sometimes during the night she woke and found him
asleep there and the child sleeping, too.

The coffee was good but too little. Outside
everything shivered in tinfoil — only the clover

between the cobblestones hung stubbornly on,
green as an afterthought....

Motherhood

She dreams the baby's so small she keeps
misplacing it — it rolls from the hutch
and the mouse carries it home, it disappears
with his shirt in the wash.
Then she drops it and it explodes
like a watermelon, eyes spitting.

Finally they get to the countryside;
Thomas has it in a sling.
He's strewing rice along the road
while the trees chitter with tiny birds.
In the meadow to their right three men
are playing rough with a white wolf. She calls

warning but the wolf breaks free
and she runs, the rattle
rolls into the gully, then she's
there and tossing the baby behind her,
listening for its cry as she straddles
the wolf and circles its throat, counting
until her thumbs push through to the earth.
White fur seeps red. She is hardly breathing.
The small wild eyes
go opaque with confusion and shame, like a child's.

Anniversary

Twelve years to the day
he puts the blue worry bead into his mouth.
The trick is to swallow your good luck, too.
Last words to a daughter...
and a wink to remember him by.

The House on Bishop Street

No front yard to speak of,
just a porch cantilevered on faith
where she arranged the canary's cage.
The house stayed dark all year
though there was instant light and water.
(No more gas jets hissing,

their flicker glinting off
Anna Rettich's midwife spectacles
as she whispered *think a baby*
and the babies came.) Spring
brought a whiff of cherries, the kind
you boiled for hours in sugar and cloves

from the yard of the Jewish family next door.
Yumanski refused to speak so
she never bought his vegetables
at the Canal Street Market. Gertrude,
his youngest and blondest,
slipped by mornings for bacon and grits.
There were summer floods and mildew

humming through fringe, there was
a picture of a ship she passed
on her way to the porch, strangers calling
from the street *Ma'am, your bird
shore can sing!* If she leaned out she could glimpse
the faintest of mauve — no more than an idea —
growing just behind the last houses.

Daystar

She wanted a little room for thinking:
but she saw diapers steaming on the line,
a doll slumped behind the door.

So she lugged a chair behind the garage
to sit out the children's naps.

Sometimes there were things to watch —
the pinched armor of a vanished cricket,
a floating maple leaf. Other days
she stared until she was assured
when she closed her eyes
she'd see only her own vivid blood.

She had an hour, at best, before Liza appeared
pouting from the top of the stairs.
And just *what* was mother doing
out back with the field mice? Why,

building a palace. Later
that night when Thomas rolled over and
lurched into her, she would open her eyes
and think of the place that was hers
for an hour — where
she was nothing,
pure nothing, in the middle of the day.

Obedience

That smokestack, for instance,
in the vacant lot across the street:
if she could order it down and watch
it float in lapse-time over buckled tar and macadam
it would stop an inch or two perhaps
before her patent leather shoes.

Her body's no longer tender, but her mind is free.
She can think up a twilight, sulfur
flicking orange then black
as the tip of a flamingo's wing, the white
picket fence marching up the hill...

but she would never create such puny stars.
The house, shut up like a pocket watch,
those tight hearts breathing inside —
she could never invent them.

The Great Palaces of Versailles

Nothing nastier than a white person!
She mutters as she irons alterations
in the backroom of Charlotte's Dress Shoppe.
The steam rising from a cranberry wool
comes alive with perspiration
and stale Evening of Paris.
Swamp she born from, swamp
she swallow, swamp she got to sink again.

The iron shoves gently
into a gusset, waits until
the puckers bloom away. Beyond
the curtain, the white girls are all
wearing shoulder pads to make their faces
delicate. That laugh would be Autumn,
tossing her hair in imitation of Bacall.

Beulah had read in the library
how French ladies at court would tuck
their fans in a sleeve
and walk in the gardens for air. Swaying
among lilies, lifting shy layers of silk,
they dropped excrement as daintily
as handkerchieves. Against all rules

she had saved the lining from a botched coat
to face last year's gray skirt. She knows
whenever she lifts a knee
she flashes crimson. That seems legitimate;
but in the book she had read
how the *cavaliere* amused themselves
wearing powder and perfume and spraying

yellow borders knee-high on the stucco
of the *Orangerie*.

A hanger clatters
in the front of the shoppe.
Beulah remembers how
even Autumn could lean into a settee
with her ankles crossed, sighing
I need a man who'll protect me
while smoking her cigarette down to the very end.

Pomade

She sweeps the kitchen floor of the river bed her husband saw fit
to bring home with his catfish, recalling
a flower — very straight,
with a spiked collar arching
under a crown of bright fluffy worms —
she had gathered in armfuls
along a still road in Tennessee. Even then
he was forever off in the woods somewhere in search
of a magic creek.

It was Willemma shushed the pack of dusty children
and took her inside the leaning cabin with its little
window in the door, the cutout magazine cloud taped to the pane
so's I'll always have shade. It was Willemma
showed her how to rub the petals fine
and heat them slow in mineral oil
until the skillet exhaled pears and nuts and rotting fir.

That cabin leaned straight away
to the south, took the very slant of heaven
through the crabgrass and Queen Anne's Lace to
the Colored Cemetery down in Wartrace. Barley soup
yearned toward the bowl's edge, the cornbread
hot from the oven climbed in glory
to the very black lip of the cast iron pan...
but Willemma stood straight as the day
she walked five miles to town for Scotch tape
and back again. Gaslight flickered on the cockeyed surface

of rain water in a galvanized pail in the corner
while Thomas pleaded with his sister
to get out while she still was fit.

Beebalm. The fragrance always put her
in mind of Turkish minarets against
a sky wrenched blue,
sweet and merciless. Willemma could wear her gray hair twisted
in two knots at the temples and still smell like travel.
But all those years she didn't budge. She simply turned
one day from slicing a turnip into a pot
when her chest opened and the inrushing air
knocked her down. *Call the reverend, I'm in the floor*
she called out to a passerby.

Beulah gazes through the pale speckled linoleum
to the webbed loam with its salt and worms. She smooths
her hair, then sniffs her palms. On the countertop
the catfish grins
like an oriental gentleman. Nothing ever stops. She feels
herself slowly rolling down the sides of the earth.

Headddress

The hat on the table
in the dining room
is no pet trained
to sit still. Three
pearl-tipped spears and Beulah
maneuvering her shadow
to the floor. The hat
is cold. The hat
wants more.

(The customer will be
generous when satisfied
beyond belief. Spangled
tulle, then, in green
and gold and sherry.)

Beulah
would have settled
for less. She doesn't
pray when she's
terrified, sometimes, in-
side her skin like
today, humming
through a mouthful of pins.

Finished it's a mountain
on a dish, a capitol
poised on a littered shore.
The brim believes

in itself, its
double rose and feathers
ashiver. Extravagance
redeems. O
intimate parasol
that teaches to walk
with grace along beauty's seam.

Sunday Greens

She wants to hear
wine pouring.
She wants to taste
change. She wants
pride to roar through
the kitchen till it shines
like straw, she wants

lean to replace
tradition. Ham knocks
in the pot, nothing
but bones, each
with its bracelet
of flesh.

The house stinks
like a zoo in summer,
while upstairs
her man sleeps on.
Robe slung over
her arm and
the cradled hymnal,

she pauses, remembers
her mother in a slip
lost in blues,
and those collards,
wild-eared,
singing.

Recovery

He's tucked his feet into corduroy scuffs
and gone out to the porch. From the parlor
with its glassed butterflies, the mandolin on the wall,
she can see one bare heel bobbing.

Years ago he had promised to take her to Chicago.
He was lovely then, a pigeon
whose pulse could be seen when the moment
was perfectly still. In the house

the dark rises and whirrs like a loom.
She stands by the davenport,
obedient among her trinkets,
secrets like birdsong in the air.

Nightmare

She's dreaming
of salt again:
salt stinging her eyes,
making pepper of her hair,
salt in her panties
and the light all over.
If she wakes
she'll find him
gone and the dog
barking its tail off,
locked outside in the
dead of night.

Lids pinched shut,
she forces the itching
away. That streetlamp
through the window:
iridescent grit. As a girl
she once opened
an umbrella in the house
and her mother cried
you'll ruin us!
but that was so
long ago. Then
she wakes up.

Wingfoot Lake

(Independence Day, 1964)

On her 36th birthday, Thomas had shown her
her first swimming pool. It had been
his favorite color, exactly — just
so much of it, the swimmers' white arms jutting
into the chevrons of high society.
She had rolled up her window
and told him to drive on, fast.

Now this *act of mercy*: four daughters
dragging her to their husbands' company picnic,
white families on one side and them
on the other, unpacking the same
squeeze bottles of Heinz, the same
waxy beef patties and Salem potato chip bags.
So he was dead for the first time
on Fourth of July — ten years ago

had been harder, waiting for something to happen,
and ten years before that, the girls
like young horses eyeing the track.
Last August she stood alone for hours
in front of the T.V. set
as a crow's wing moved slowly through
the white streets of government.
That brave swimming

scared her, like Joanna saying
Mother, we're Afro-Americans now!
What did she know about Africa?
Were there lakes like this one

with a rowboat pushed under the pier?
Or Thomas' Great Mississippi
with its sullen silks? (There was
the Nile but the Nile belonged

to God.) Where she came from
was the past, 12 miles into town
where nobody had locked their back door,
and Goodyear hadn't begun to dream of a park
under the company symbol, a white foot
sprouting two small wings.

Company

No one can help him anymore.
Not the young thing next door
in the red pedal pushers,
not the canary he drove distracted

with his mandolin. There'll be
no more trees to wake him in moonlight,
nor a single dry spring morning
when the fish are lonely for company.

She's standing there telling him: give it up.
She is weary of sirens and his face
worn with salt. *If this is code,*

she tells him, *listen: we were good,*
though we never believed it.
And now he can't even touch her feet.

The Oriental Ballerina

twirls on the tips of a carnation
while the radio scratches out a morning hymn.
Daylight has not ventured as far

as the windows — the walls are still dark,
shadowed with the ghosts
of oversized gardenias. The ballerina

pirouettes to the wheeze of the old
rugged cross, she lifts
her shoulders past the edge

of the jewelbox lid. Two pink slippers
touch the ragged petals, no one
should have feet that small! In China

they do everything upside down:
this ballerina has not risen but drilled
a tunnel straight to America

where the bedrooms of the poor
are papered in vulgar flowers
on a background the color of grease, of

teabags, of cracked imitation walnut veneer.
On the other side of the world
they are shedding robes sprigged with

roses, roses drifting with a hiss
to the floor by the bed
as, here, the sun finally strikes the windows

suddenly opaque,
noncommital as shields. In this room
is a bed where the sun has gone

walking. Where a straw nods over
the lip of its glass and a hand
reaches for a tissue, crumpling it to a flower.

The ballerina had been drilling all night!
She flaunts her skirts like sails,
whirling in a disk so bright,

so rapidly she is standing still.
The sun walks the bed to the pillow
and pauses for breath (in the Orient,

breath floats like mist
in the fields), hesitating
at a knotted handkerchief that has slid

on its string and has lodged beneath
the right ear which discerns
the most fragile music

where there is none. The ballerina dances
at the end of a tunnel of light,
she spins on her impossible toes —

the rest is shadow.
The head on the pillow sees nothing
else, though it feels the sun warming

its cheeks. *There is no China;*
no cross, just the papery kiss
of a kleenex above the stink of camphor,

the walls exploding with shabby tutus....

Chronology

1900:   Thomas born in Wartrace, Tennessee.

1904:   Beulah born in Rockmart, Georgia.

1906:   Beulah's family moves to Akron.

1916:   30,000 workers migrate to Akron.

1919:   Thomas leaves Tennessee for the riverboat life.

1921:   Thomas arrives in Akron.

1922:   Completion of viaduct spanning the Little Cuyahoga River.

1924:   December wedding.

1926:   First child born (Rose).

1928:   New car bought for the trip to Tennessee.

1929:   The Goodyear Zeppelin Airdock is built — the largest building in the world without interior supports.

1930:   Lose car due to The Depression. Second child born (Agnes).

1931:   The airship *Akron* disaster.

1932:   Vice-President of First Central Trust Company commits suicide. A union organizer is killed trying to aid an evicted family.

1932:   November: Third child born (Liza).

1934:   Part-time work cleaning offices of the Satisfaction Coal Company.

1935:   Fourth child born (Joanna). They move to Bishop Street.

1940:	11,000 Negroes living in Akron (total population: 243,000).
1942:	Thomas employed at Goodyear Aircraft in war relief work.
1945:	Rose marries a war veteran.
1946:	Thomas quits the gospel choir at the A.M.E. Zion Church.
1946:	Beulah takes a part-time job in Charlotte's Dress Shoppe.
1947:	First grandchild (Pauline) born to Rose.
1949:	Second grandchild (Jacqueline) born to Rose.
1950:	Beulah takes up millinery.
1951:	The only grandson (Malcolm) born to Agnes.
1956:	All daughters have been married off.
1960:	Thomas has first heart attack.
1963:	April: Thomas dies.
1963:	August: The March on Washington.
1964:	Beulah's daughters invite her to a Fourth of July picnic.
1966:	Beulah inflicted with glaucoma. She takes to her bed.
1969:	April: Beulah dies.

RITA DOVE was born in Akron, Ohio, in 1952 and was educated at Miami University, Universität Tübingen (West Germany), and the University of Iowa. A recipient of fellowships from the National Endowment for the Arts and the John Simon Guggenheim Memorial Foundation, she has been writer-in-residence at Tuskegee Institute and presently teaches at Arizona State University.